YOU MI...HIS...

1902

MILESTONES, MEMORIES,
TRIVIA AND FACTS, NEWS EVENTS,
PROMINENT PERSONALITIES &
SPORTS HIGHLIGHTS OF THE YEAR

TO :

FROM :

MESSAGE :

*selected and researched
by
mary a. pradt*

WARNER **W** TREASURES ™

PUBLISHED BY WARNER BOOKS

A TIME WARNER COMPANY

Warner Books, Inc.
1271 Avenue of the Americas
New York, New York 10020

Warner Treasures is a
trademark of Warner Books, Inc.

 A Time Warner Company

DESIGN:
CAROL BOKUNIEWICZ DESIGN
PRINTED IN SINGAPORE
FIRST PRINTING : MAY 1995
10 9 8 7 6 5 4 3 2 1
ISBN : 0-446-91038-4

On Christmas 1962, according to the census clock, the U.S. population reached 188 million, a gain of 2,710,000 over January 1, 1962.

Lt. Col. John H. Glenn, Jr., was the first American to orbit the earth, in a Mercury spacecraft, the Friendship 7, in February. The launch had been plagued with delays and fears. U.S. confidence in the space program got a jump start. Hundreds of thousands of spectators flocked to Florida beaches, and millions more watched TV coverage. President Kennedy flew to Cape Canaveral to present Glenn with a medal and praise his "unflinching courage" and "extraordinary ability." In New York, Glenn, his family, and fellow astronauts got a ticker tape parade down Broadway's Canyon of Heroes that broke all records since the end of WWII.

2

The Kennedys dominated the headlines. Jackie led an hour-long televised tour of the White House in February; CBS and NBC carried it simultaneously. Millions of viewers were transfixed by glimpses into the restoration of the historic building. Jackie was poised and well informed in her narration. She was dazzling in a simple light-colored wool suit and three strands of pearls.

newsreel

THE SUPREME COURT, ON JUNE 25, HELD (6–1) THAT THE READING OF AN OFFICIAL PRAYER IN NEW YORK PUBLIC SCHOOLS VIOLATED THE FIRST AMENDMENT.

JFK's biggest trial was the **Cuban missile crisis**—for one week in October 1962, we thought war might be imminent, over the Soviet military buildup in Cuba. The U.S. had revealed reconnaissance photos of missile sites in Cuba and put up a blockade around the island, a "quarantine" that lasted a month. Khrushchev backed down, promising to remove missiles and dismantle bases. There was a collective sigh of relief.

Pope John XXIII opened the Vatican Council on October 11, with 2,700 Roman Catholic prelates present. The ecumenical council was an ambitious attempt by the church to confront modern dilemmas.

In June, an Air France Boeing 707 crashed at Paris, killing 130 persons; the death toll was the worst single-plane disaster in aviation history.

Adolf Eichmann was hanged in Israel on May 31. He had been convicted of war crimes in the Nazi slaughter of millions of Jews during World War II.

PETER FECHTER, 18, WAS THE FIRST MAN KILLED TRYING TO DEFECT OVER THE SIX-FOOT-HIGH BERLIN WALL, ON AUGUST 17.

The USSR in August put two manned spacecraft in orbit, to fly in tandem. It was widely suspected that this was part of a long-range Soviet plan to put a man on the moon.

headlines

international

WAR BROKE OUT BETWEEN INDIA AND CHINA, WITH CHINA THE EASY WINNER.

Charles de Gaulle survived the second assassination attempt in a year in August. The underground Secret Army Organization (O.A.S.) struck widely in France to oppose de Gaulle's Algerian policies. Algeria was declared independent in July after 132 years of French colonial rule.

From December 3 to 7, a famous killer fog enveloped London. More than 100 deaths occurred, mostly due to the abnormally high sulfur dioxide levels in the air.

The shopping center was replacing the courthouse square as the center of a town's recreational and cultural life. Pop concerts, fashion shows, bowling, cooking schools, and folk dance classes all took place at the mall. Movie theaters at the mall were a big trend—of 183 new hardtop (non–drive-in) theaters built in the previous 2 years, 63 were located in shopping centers. Downtown movie theaters and drive-ins were shuttering. Fortunately, some of the big drive-in chains had the sense to switch their emphasis to shopping center movie houses.

The first worldwide TV transmission, via Telstar satellite, occurred July 11. It included a seven-minute feed from France, with an Yves Montand song, and test patterns and a government greeting from Britain.

cultural
milestones

THE NEW YORK PHILHARMONIC, UNDER LEONARD BERNSTEIN, OPENED PHILHARMONIC HALL IN NEW YORK'S LINCOLN CENTER.

On Broadway, *I Can Get It for You Wholesale* opened March 22, with Elliott Gould, Lillian Roth, Sheree North, and Barbra Streisand among the cast. Edward Albee's important *Who's Afraid of Virginia Woolf?* opened October 13.

BEN CASEY

Johnny Carson took over as host of "The Tonight Show" October 1. Jack Paar premiered on late-night TV. Jackie Gleason returned in "The Jackie Gleason Show: The American Scene Magazine" on CBS. Even Jack ("dum-de-dum-dum") Webb was back in an early example of tabloid TV, retelling tales from the files of *True* magazine. Walter Cronkite replaced Douglas Edwards as CBS News anchor April 16.

President Kennedy signed a bill May 1 authorizing $33 million for the expansion of public television.

television

TOP-RATED TV SHOWS OF 1962

1. "The Beverly Hillbillies" (CBS)
2. "Candid Camera" (CBS)
3. "The Red Skelton Show" (CBS)
4. "Bonanza" (NBC)
5. "The Lucy Show" (CBS)
6. "The Andy Griffith Show" (CBS)
7. "Ben Casey" (ABC)
8. "The Danny Thomas Show" (CBS)
9. "The Dick Van Dyke Show" (CBS)
10. "Gunsmoke" (CBS)

Rounding out the top 20:

"Dr. Kildare" (NBC)
"The Jack Benny Show" (CBS)
"What's My Line?" (CBS)
"The Ed Sullivan Show" (CBS)
"Hazel" (NBC)
"I've Got A Secret" (CBS)
"The Jackie Gleason Show" (CBS)
"The Defenders" (CBS)
"To Tell the Truth" (CBS)
and "Lassie" on CBS of course.

ON NBC, "THE JETSONS" PREMIERED.

"The Beverly Hillbillies" was the runaway hit of the season. The Clampetts, a family of Ozark hicks who struck oil, led by Pa (Buddy Ebsen), moved to Beverly Hills; very high concept. Culture shock ensued. Pa looked over the mansion's vast lawn and announced, "We'll commence plowing tomorrow." "But this is Beverly Hills," objected the banker. "Dirt is dirt," observed Pa. Or, Granny: "Them pigs got into the corn." Pa: "Did they drink much?"

celeb weddings:

Prince Juan Carlos Alfonso Víctor María de Borbón y Borbón, 24, the son of the Spanish pretender Don Juan, and **Princess Sophia of the Hellenes**, daughter of King Paul and Queen Frederika of Greece, were married in Athens May 14. Sophia had relinquished her rights to succession to the Greek throne. In 1975, Juan Carlos would be proclaimed king days after the death of Generalissimo Francisco Franco.

Lotte Lenya, 64, widow of Kurt (*The Threepenny Opera*) Weill, married American impressionist painter **Russell Detwiler**, 37. "When you are really in love, age just becomes something written in your passport."

Edith Piaf, 47, the tragic French chanteuse, married **Theo Sarapo**, 23, a former hairdresser who became Piaf's singing protégé.

HERSCHEL WALKER, football player who also practiced ballet, was born March 3.

DARRYL STRAWBERRY, baseball player with the stunning smile, was born March 12.

WILLIAM "REFRIGERATOR" PERRY, the fattest man in football, was born on December 16.

DEMI MOORE, notorious *Vanity Fair* cover girl and actress, was born on November 11.

KRISTY MCNICHOL, TV and film actress, was born on September 9.

DON MATTINGLY, New York Yankees first baseman, was born April 20.

RALPH MACCHIO, the *Karate Kid* actor, was born November 4.

JACKIE JOYNER-KERSEE, Olympic heptathlete, was born March 3.

BO JACKSON, professional football and baseball player, was born November 30.

DEATHS

Ernie Kovacs, an important influence on TV comedy, star of his own show featuring such skits as Percy Dovetonsils and the Nairobi Trio, was killed at 42 in a car crash January 13 in West L.A. He and his wife, singer Edie Adams, had driven separate cars from a baby shower for Mrs. Milton Berle at the home of Billy Wilder.

William Faulkner, the Pulitzer and Nobel Prize–winning novelist, died July 6 in Oxford, MS, at 64.

milestones

GENIE FRANCIS, famous for her role as Laura in "General Hospital," was born May 26.

JODIE FOSTER, actress and director, was born November 19.

PATRICK EWING, New York Knicks center, was born August 5.

EMILIO ESTEVEZ, Brat Pack actor, was born May 12.

CLYDE DREXLER, nicknamed "The Glide" and a Portland Trailblazer, was born June 22.

ERIC DAVIS, baseball player, was born May 29.

TOM CRUISE, hunky film actor, was born July 3.

ROGER CLEMENS, Boston Red Sox pitcher known for striking out 20 players in one game, was born August 4.

MATTHEW BRODERICK, actor, was born March 21.

JON BON JOVI (BONGIOVI), musician, was born March 2.

TRACY AUSTIN, bouncy tennis player, was born December 12.

PAULA ABDUL, singer, dancer, and choreographer, was born June 19.

Marilyn Monroe was found dead of barbiturate overdose at 36, on August 5, 1962.

Eleanor Roosevelt, widow of FDR, reformer, author, and UN envoy, died. Presidents Kennedy, Truman, and Eisenhower attended her November 10 funeral at Hyde Park, NY.

e(dward) e(stlin) cummings, 67, American poet, died in September.

Herman Hesse, Nobel winner and serious thinker best remembered for *Siddhartha* and for *Steppenwolf*, a classic that was renounced by the Hitler regime and is still widely read today, died at 85.

1. **i can't stop loving you** Ray Charles

2. **big girls don't cry** Four Seasons

3. **sherry** Four Seasons

4. **roses are red (my love)** Bobby Vinton

5. **peppermint twist—part 1** Joey Dee & the Starliters

6. **telstar** Tornadoes

7. **soldier boy** Shirelles

8. **hey! baby** Bruce Channel

hit music

Also in the top 20:

johnny angel Shelley Fabares

he's a rebel Crystals

breaking up is hard to do Neil Sedaka

monster mash Bobby "Boris" Pickett

good luck charm Elvis Presley

sheila Tommy Roe

stranger on the shore Mr. Acker Bilk

the stripper David Rose

9. **duke of earl** Gene Chandler

10. **the twist** Chubby Checker

12

CHUBBY CHECKER

fiction

1. **ship of fools**
   katherine anne porter

2. **dearly beloved**
   anne morrow lindbergh

3. **a shade of difference**
   allen drury

4. **youngblood hawke**
   herman wouk

5. **franny and zooey**
   j. d. salinger

6. **fail-safe**
   eugene burdick and
   harvey wheeler

7. **seven days in may**
   fletcher knebel and
   charles w. bailey II

8. **the prize**
   irving wallace

9. **the agony and
   the ecstasy**
   irving stone

10. **the reivers**
    william faulkner

bestselling

books

Arnold Palmer won the Masters golf tournament, beating Gary Player and Dow Finsterwald in April in a three-way playoff. South African Gary Player won the PGA tourney in July. Jack Nicklaus beat Arnold Palmer by three strokes in a playoff at the U.S. Open in June; he had just turned pro in January.

The baseball season was rather a comedy of errors. The new NL team, the New York Mets, under Casey Stengel, former Yankee manager, lost 120 of their 160 games. The fans, however, loved them; nearly one million turned out for their disastrous first season. The Houston Astros were the other new franchise. One three-game playoff between the transplanted Bums and Jints—i.e. the L.A. Dodgers and S.F. Giants—was viewed with horror by 20 million on TV. The hitting was atrocious, there were 11 errors, the second game lasted 4 hours and 18 minutes and used up a record 42 players, and the umpires became tongue-tied and amnesiac.

Horse racing enjoyed great popularity. Attendance was up over 1961, and betting was up 5.57 %. Kelso was the horse of the year for the third year, er, running. The 88th Kentucky Derby was won by Decidedly, with Bill Hartack up. Green Money won the Preakness, and Jaipur prevailed in the Belmont Stakes, with Willie Shoemaker up. Eddie Arcaro, considered the greatest modern jockey, retired after a 31-year career, in which he rode 4,779 winners and won purses totaling more than $30 million.

Boxing It was embarrassing when Sonny Liston, an ex-con, knocked out defending world heavyweight champ Floyd Patterson only 2 minutes and 6 seconds into the first round. Boxing was already under a cloud, and it wasn't getting any sunnier.

The Boston Celtics won their fourth consecutive NBA championship in April. The first basketball player to score 100 points in a game was Wilt Chamberlain, Philly Warriors' star, who made 36 goals and 28 foul shots in a game against the NY Knicks March 2.

sports

Pro football was established as the spectator sport of the sixties—and this was before the first Super Bowl. Baseball, although the "national sport," could be boring. The apocryphal line of the time: "There's an insomniac in Manhattan who gave up Seconal for the Yankees." The conquering heroes of pro football were the Green Bay Packers, led by the legendary Vince Lombardi. "The Pack" bested the New York Giants in the NFL championship, 16–7, second year running. The Dallas Texans beat the Houston Oilers 20–17 in the AFL championship; Tommy Brooker's field goal in the second extra quarter decided the game. Terry Baker, QB of Oregon State, won the Heisman Trophy.

17

Lawrence of Arabia won for Best Picture over *The Longest Day*, *The Music Man*, *Mutiny on the Bounty*, and *To Kill a Mockingbird*. *Lawrence* also took Oscars for Best Director (**David Lean**), color cinematography, color art direction, and best original musical score (a new classification this year, won by **Maurice Jarre**). **Gregory Peck** was named Best Actor for his *Mockingbird* role, over Burt Lancaster in *Birdman of Alcatraz*, Jack Lemmon in *Days of Wine and Roses*, Marcello Mastroianni in *Divorce—Italian Style*, and Peter O'Toole as T. E. Lawrence of Arabia. **Anne Bancroft** got Best Actress honors for *The Miracle Worker*, and **Patty Duke**, her costar, was named Best Supporting Actress. Bancroft beat Bette Davis in *Whatever Happened to Baby Jane?*, Katharine Hepburn, who starred in the screen version of *Long Day's Journey into Night*, Geraldine Page in *Sweet Bird of Youth*, and Lee Remick in *Days of Wine and Roses*. **Ed Begley** got the Supporting Actor award for *Sweet Bird of Youth*. Other nominees were Victor Buono, Telly Savalas (*Birdman*), Omar Sharif (*Lawrence*), and Terence Stamp. Patty Duke won over Mary Badham, Shirley Knight, Angela Lansbury, and Thelma Ritter. Best Foreign Language Film was **Sundays and Cybèle**. Best Song honors went to **Henry Mancini and Johnny Mercer** for the theme from *Days of Wine and Roses*.

18

Top box-office films of the year:
1. **Spartacus** earned $13,500,000 at the box office
2. **West Side Story** about $11 million
3. **Lover Come Back**
4. **That Touch of Mink**
5. **El Cid**
6. **The Music Man**
7. **King of Kings**
8. **Hatari**
9. **Flower Drum Song**
10. **The Interns**

Lawrence of Arabia was released just in time for the Oscar nominations, not soon enough to be a top earner in 1962—it would be in 1963, however.